316

THE KITCHEN LIBRARY

CAKE ICING &

DECORATING

THE KITCHEN LIBRARY

CAKE ICING & DECORATING

Carole Handslip

HAMLYN

CONTENTS

This edition published in 1990 by
The Hamlyn Publishing Group Limited,
a division of the Octopus Publishing Group,
Michelin House, 81 Fulham Road,
London SW3 6RB

© Cathay Books 1981

ISBN 0 600 56936 5

Produced by Mandarin Offset
Printed and Bound in Hong Kong

INTRODUCTION

Cake decorating is a fascinating and rewarding craft. This handbook shows you just how simple it can be, and encourages those of you who have the basic skills to try something more elaborate.

Beginning with simple butter icings, each chapter takes you step-by-step through icing techniques, progressing to designing and royal icing a wedding cake. Each chapter provides a selection of cake recipes, using the techniques described within the chapter.

Step-by-step photographs show you how to make a variety of cake decorations, including piped flowers, chocolate shapes, marzipan fruits and Christmas cake decorations. Many of these decorations can be prepared in advance and stored until required – to avoid a last minute rush.

Some of the cakes – especially the royal iced ones and more elaborate novelty cakes – take time to complete but you will find this absorbing hobby satisfying. By practising the techniques in each chapter and following the suggested designs you should be able to produce a professional cake for every occasion.

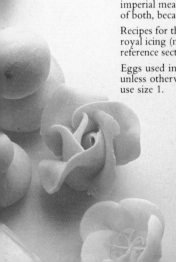

NOTES

Standard spoon measurements are used in all recipes
1 tablespoon = one 15 ml spoon
1 teaspoon = one 5 ml spoon
All spoon measures are level.

Ovens should be preheated to the specified temperature.

For all recipes, quantities are given in both metric and imperial measures. Follow either set but not a mixture of both, because they are not inter-changeable.

Recipes for the basic cake mixtures, almond paste and royal icing (marked with asterisks) are given in the reference section (pages 86-91).

Eggs used in the recipes are standard size, i.e. size 3, unless otherwise stated. If large eggs are specified, use size 1.

Basic Decorating Equipment

You will probably find that you already have most of the basic equipment needed for simple cake decorating.

Several *mixing bowls* and *small basins* are needed when working with different coloured icings.

A *sieve* is necessary for sifting icing sugar to ensure that there are no lumps in the icing.

A *spatula* enables you to scrape every last bit of icing out of a bowl and avoids wastage.

A small and a medium sized *palette knife* are a great help when spreading icing over the top of the cake and round the sides.

Piping nozzles for simple icings are usually larger than those used for royal icing. A 5 mm (1/4 inch) and a 1 cm (1/2 inch) 8-cut rose nozzle will probably be sufficient for use with butter icings. A No. 2 writing nozzle is useful for piping glacé icing and melted chocolate.

Nylon piping bags are necessary for piping butter icings.

Greaseproof paper piping bags are best for piping melted chocolate and glacé icing.

Fine paintbrushes are used for painting food colourings onto icings and moulded decorations.

A *sugar thermometer* is essential when making American frosting and fondant icings. Stand it in hot water for a few minutes before and after use. Clean and dry thoroughly.

A *cake board*, or a thinner *cake card*, enhances an iced cake but is not essential; a large flat plate can be used if liked. Cake boards and cards may be used again: just wipe them over with a damp cloth and leave to dry – do not wash them.

As you become more interested and wish to achieve better results, there are additional pieces of equipment that will help you. These are described in the chapter on royal icing.

To Make a Greaseproof Paper Piping Bag

A greaseproof paper piping bag is the simplest to use for royal icing. Make several at a time if you are using different piping nozzles or several colourings, or icing a large cake.

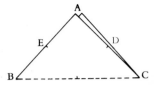

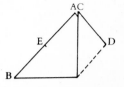

1. Fold a 25 cm (10 inch) square of greaseproof paper in half to form a triangle.

2. Fold point C to point A on a flat surface and crease well.

3. Fold point D over to point E and crease well.

4. Fold point A to point B and crease well.

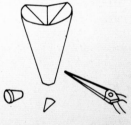

5. Hold the bag where points D and E meet. Shape into a cone, overlap points twice and crease to secure.

6. Cut off the tip of the cone and insert a nozzle. Do not fill more than half full.

SIMPLE ICINGS & DECORATIONS

Cake decorating can be as simple as sprinkling icing sugar onto a cake through a d'oyley or strips of paper. Glacé icing the top of a cake and applying bought sweets or other decorations when dry is another simple idea.

The sides of a cake can be left plain but they look more attractive if covered with butter icing or apricot glaze and then rolled in toasted or coloured coconut, nuts, or a similar coating. If the sides are coated, decorate the top edge of the cake with smarties, chocolate drops, or nuts to finish it off neatly. For a more decorative finish, pipe butter icing around the edge.

Individual cup cakes are quick to make and easy to decorate effectively. Top them with glacé icing, then apply sweets, nuts or cherries and angelica, or mark a feather design on the icing (see page 15).

Glacé Icing

250 g (8 oz) icing
    sugar
2 tablespoons warm
    water
    (approximately)
flavouring (see
    below) or few
    drops of food
    colouring
    (optional)

Sift the icing sugar into a mixing bowl and gradually add the water. The icing should be thick enough to coat the back of the spoon thickly. Add the flavouring or colouring and use immediately.

This quantity is sufficient to ice 18 to 24 small cakes. A half-quantity will ice the top of a 20 cm (8 inch) round cake.

Makes a 250 g (8 oz) mixture

FLAVOURINGS

Coffee: Replace 1 tablespoon warm water with 1 tablespoon coffee essence.

Orange or lemon: Replace 1 table-spoon warm water with 1 tablespoon orange or lemon juice. Add the grated rind of 1 orange or lemon and a few drops of food colouring.

Chocolate: Sift 3 tablespoons cocoa with the icing sugar.

Crème au Beurre

2 egg whites
125 g (4 oz) icing
  sugar, sifted
125 g (4 oz)
  unsalted butter
flavouring (see
  below) or few
  drops of food
  colouring
  (optional)

Place the egg whites and icing sugar in a mixing bowl over a pan of simmering water and whisk until the mixture holds its shape. Cool slightly. Cream the butter until soft then beat in the meringue mixture a little at a time. Flavour or colour as desired.

This quantity is sufficient to fill and ice the top of a 20 cm (8 inch) sandwich cake.

If stored in an airtight container, this icing can be kept in the refrigerator for several weeks.

Makes a 125 g (4 oz) mixture

FLAVOURINGS

Chocolate: Melt 50 g (2 oz) plain chocolate in a bowl over a pan of hot water. Cool and beat in with the meringue mixture.

Coffee: Add 1 tablespoon coffee essence with the meringue mixture.

Praline: Add 3 tablespoons crushed Praline (see page 14) with the meringue mixture.

Butter Icing

125 g (4 oz) butter
250 g (8 oz) icing
    sugar, sifted
2 tablespoons milk
flavouring (see
    below) or few
    drops of food
    colouring
    (optional)

Beat the butter with half the icing sugar until smooth. Add remaining icing sugar with the milk and flavouring. Beat until creamy.

This quantity is sufficient to fill and cover a 20 cm (8 inch) sandwich cake.

If stored in an airtight container, this icing can be kept in the refrigerator for several weeks.

Makes a 250 g (8 oz) mixture

FLAVOURINGS

Lemon or orange: Add the grated rind of 1 lemon or orange to the butter. Replace the milk with lemon or orange juice. Add a few drops of yellow or orange colouring.

Mocha: Blend 1 teaspoon cocoa powder and 2 teaspoons instant coffee powder with 1 tablespoon boiling water. Cool, then add to the mixture with only 1 tablespoon milk.

Chocolate: Blend 2 tablespoons cocoa powder with 2 tablespoons boiling water. Cool, then add to the mixture with only 1 tablespoon milk.

Coffee: Replace 1 tablespoon milk with 1 tablespoon coffee essence.

American Frosting

250 g (8 oz)
  granulated sugar
4 tablespoons water
pinch of cream of
  tartar
1 egg white

Put the sugar and water in a heavy-based pan and heat gently, stirring occasionally, until dissolved.

Add the cream of tartar and bring to the boil without stirring. Boil for 10 minutes or until the syrup registers 115°C (240°F) on a sugar thermometer.

Meanwhile, whisk the egg white until very stiff. Pour the sugar syrup in a thin stream onto the egg white, whisking all the time. Continue to whisk until the frosting stands in stiff peaks, with the tips just falling.

Spoon the icing onto the centre of the cake and spread over the top and sides, working quickly as the icing soon starts to set. Form into swirls or peaks with a palette knife.

Place any decorations in position while the icing is still soft. The icing forms a crisp crust but remains soft underneath.

This quantity is sufficient to cover an 18 cm (7 inch) round cake.

Makes a 250 g (8 oz) mixture

Caramel Frosting

175 g (6 oz) soft
  brown sugar
1 egg white
2 tablespoons hot
  water
pinch of cream of
  tartar

Put all the ingredients in a bowl over a pan of hot water and whisk for 5 to 7 minutes until thick. Use immediately, forming into swirls on the cake with a palette knife.

This quantity is sufficient to fill and cover a 20 cm (8 inch) round cake.

Makes a 175 g (6 oz) mixture

VARIATION

Mock Frosting: Replace the brown sugar with caster sugar. This can be used as a substitute for American frosting if you do not have a sugar thermometer.

Chocolate Fudge Icing

50 g (2 oz) butter
3 tablespoons milk
250 g (8 oz) icing
    sugar, sifted
2 tablespoons cocoa
    powder, sifted

Melt the butter in a small saucepan with the milk. Add the icing sugar and cocoa and beat well until smooth and glossy. Leave until lukewarm, then pour over the cake.

    This quantity is sufficient to fill and ice the top of a 20 cm (8 inch) sandwich cake.

Makes a 250 g (8 oz) mixture

NOTE: If the icing is too thick to pour, reheat gently to thin.

SIMPLE DECORATIONS

To decorate the sides: Apply a layer of butter icing, or brush with apricot glaze.

To make apricot glaze: Place 250 g (8 oz) apricot jam and 3 tablespoons water in a small pan and heat until dissolved. Add a squeeze of lemon juice, then sieve and return to the pan. Bring to the boil and simmer until syrupy. Use warm. The glaze can be stored in the refrigerator for several months; reheat gently to use.

To apply the coating: Place on a sheet of grease-proof paper. Hold cake between the palms of the hands and roll lightly in the coating until evenly covered. Grated chocolate, crushed corn-flakes, hundreds and thousands, and chocolate strands are simple but effective. Chopped or flaked nuts, coloured or toasted desiccated coconut and crushed praline are also good. Flaked or chopped almonds are best toasted.

To toast coconut or almonds: Place on a baking sheet under a moderate grill for a few minutes, stirring frequently, until golden.

To colour coconut: Add a drop of food colouring and stir until evenly coloured.

Crushed praline: Gently heat 50 g (2 oz) each unblanched almonds and sugar in a small pan until the sugar browns and the almonds begin to split. Turn onto an oiled baking sheet to cool. Crush with a rolling pin. This can be stored in an airtight container for several weeks.

To decorate the top: Effective finishes can be created using butter icing or other icing with suitable texture.

1. Draw a palette knife across the icing from side to side, slightly overlapping the previous line each time (see page 23).

2. Spread a thick layer of icing over the top of the cake. Pull up into peaks with a palette knife (see page 13).

3. Using a palette knife, make swirls all round the cake, from the outside to the centre (see page 11).

4. Using a fork make a circular design all around the cake, then draw a pointed knife from the edge towards the centre in 8 places to give a scalloped effect.

Feather Icing

This gives a professional finish to glacé iced cakes. It is essential to work quickly before the icing begins to set.

Place the cake on a wire rack. Pour three-quarters of the glacé icing onto the centre of the cake and spread almost to the edge with a palette knife. Give the cake 2 or 3 sharp bangs on the table to help the icing flow to the edge. If icing drips over the edge, quickly remove with a knife or leave until set and trim. Place cake on a board.

Colour the remaining icing, spoon into a greaseproof paper piping bag fitted with a No. 1 writing nozzle. Pipe parallel lines 2.5 cm (1 inch) apart on the glacé icing.

Working quickly, draw a pointed knife vertically across the icing alternately in opposite directions at 2.5 cm

(1 inch) intervals to make a feather pattern.

Do not move the cake until the icing is set, or it may crack.

Circular Feather Design: Pipe a continuous circle on a round glacé iced cake, keeping the rings about 2.5 cm (1 inch) apart, using the contrasting colour. Draw a pointed knife from the edge to the centre, at regular intervals to create a scalloped effect.

Painted Feather Design: Onto the glacé iced cake, paint parallel lines, using food colouring and a fine paintbrush. Draw a knife across the icing alternately in opposite directions.

Simple finishes

The finishing touches can turn a simply iced cake into something special. Chocolate drops, orange and lemon slices, smarties, jelly sweets and silver balls make very attractive edgings. Whole hazelnuts and walnuts are equally effective; if the top icing is chocolate, sprinkle walnuts with icing sugar to make them white before placing them on the cake. Glacé fruits, crystallized violets and rose leaves, and sugar flowers can also be bought for finishing decorations.

If you have time, make your own decorations. Frosted fruits make a pretty home-made finish to a simple cake. Caramel chips are especially good used with caramel frosting.

A more elaborate edging can be achieved by piping butter icing into borders, rosettes or shells.

To make caramel chips: Place 175 g (6 oz) caster sugar in a small pan and heat gently until dissolved. Boil until it forms a golden caramel, then pour immediately onto a greased baking sheet and leave to cool. Break into pieces.

Frosted Fruits, Flowers and Leaves

These are quite easy to make and look most attractive. They are also edible. Frosted fruits will keep for up to 2 weeks, leaves and flowers may be kept for up to 6 weeks. Store between layers of tissue paper in an airtight container.

Small fruits such as currants, grapes and cherries are the most suitable.

Flowers with only a few petals, such as primroses, violets, campanula or rose petals, give the best results. Only use edible ones.

Leaves should be small, preferably a herb, such as mint, which also has a pleasant flavour.

Simple Frosting Method

This can be used for fruits, flowers and leaves.

1 egg white
fruit, flowers or leaves
caster sugar

Lightly whisk the egg white. Using a paint brush, lightly coat the fruit, flowers or leaves all over with the egg white. Drain or brush off any excess. Dip or dredge in caster sugar until well coated all over. Place on greaseproof paper to dry.

Gum Arabic Method

This method is not suitable for fruit.

15 g (½ oz) gum arabic
2 tablespoons rose water
flowers or leaves
caster sugar

Place the gum arabic and rose water in a screw-top jar and shake well. Leave for 2 to 3 hours, shaking occasionally, until the gum arabic has dissolved.

Paint all over the petals or leaves, covering completely. Place on grease-proof paper and leave overnight until the solution has been absorbed. Sprinkle both sides of the flower or leaf with caster sugar; shake off any surplus. Sprinkle again if necessary then leave on greaseproof paper to dry.

Chocolate Mint Cake

4-egg chocolate
    Victoria sandwich
    cake mixture*
peppermint
    flavouring
250 g (8 oz) green
    Butter icing (see
    page 11)
125 g (4 oz) green
    Glacé icing (see
    page 9)
TO DECORATE:
75 g (3 oz) chocolate
    sugar strands
50 g (2 oz) plain
    chocolate, melted

Line and grease two 20 cm (8 inch) sandwich tins. Divide the mixture between the tins and bake in a pre-heated moderate oven, 180°C (350°F), Gas Mark 4, for 25 to 30 minutes. Turn out onto a wire rack to cool.

Mix a few drops of peppermint flavouring into the butter icing. Use half to sandwich the cakes together.

Cover the sides with more icing and roll in the chocolate strands. Place on a cake board.

Put the remaining butter icing in a nylon piping bag fitted with a 5 mm (¼ inch) fluted nozzle and pipe a border around the top of the cake.

Pour the glacé icing onto the top of the cake and spread almost to the edge with a palette knife, being careful not to touch the piping. Gently bang the cake on the table 2 or 3 times to help the icing flow to the edge.

Put the melted chocolate in a greaseproof paper piping bag, cut off the tip and dribble the chocolate across the top of the cake.
Makes one 20 cm (8 inch) cake

Frosted Fruit Cake

3-egg orange-
    flavoured Whisked
    sponge cake
    mixture*
4 tablespoons
    cointreau
450 ml (¾ pint)
    double cream,
    whipped
TO DECORATE:
frosted grapes and
    mint leaves (see
    page 17)

Grease and flour a 23 cm (9 inch) ring mould. Turn the mixture into the tin and bake in a preheated moderately hot oven, 190°C (375°F), Gas Mark 5, for 30 to 35 minutes. Turn out onto a wire rack to cool.

Cut in half and sprinkle with the liqueur. Sandwich together with a quarter of the cream and place on a cake board. Cover the cake with the remaining cream and mark into a swirl pattern with a palette knife.

Arrange the frosted grapes and leaves in clusters around the top.
Makes one 23 cm (9 inch) cake

Coffee and Almond Gâteau

3-egg Whisked sponge cake mixture*
250 g (8 oz) coffee Crème au beurre (see page 10)
75 g (3 oz) flaked almonds, toasted

Line and grease a 20 × 30 cm (8 × 12 inch) Swiss roll tin. Turn the mixture into the tin and bake in a preheated moderately hot oven, 190°C (375°F), Gas Mark 5, for 20 to 25 minutes. Turn onto a wire rack to cool.

Cut the cake into 3 equal pieces and sandwich together with one third of the icing. Cover the sides with more icing and coat with the almonds. Place on a cake board.

Use a quarter of the remaining icing to cover the top of the cake, smoothing with a palette knife. Put the remaining icing in a nylon piping bag fitted, with a 5 mm (¼ inch) plain nozzle and pipe lines diagonally across the top of the gâteau.

Makes one 20 cm (8 inch) gâteau

Spider's Web Cake

4-egg chocolate
  Victoria sandwich
  cake mixture*
125 g (4 oz) coffee
  Butter icing (see
  page 11)
75 g (3 oz) walnuts,
  chopped
2 teaspoons cocoa
  powder
1 teaspoon boiling
  water
250 g (8 oz) coffee
  Glacé icing (see
  page 9)
1 tablespoon sifted
  icing sugar

Grease and line two 20 cm (8 inch) sandwich tins. Divide the mixture evenly between the tins and bake in a preheated moderate oven, 180°C (350°F), Gas Mark 4, for 25 to 30 minutes. Cool on a wire rack.

Sandwich the cakes together with three-quarters of the butter icing. Spread the rest around the side, roll in the nuts and place on a cake board.

Blend the cocoa with the boiling water. Add 3 tablespoons of the glacé icing with the icing sugar and beat well. Spoon into a greaseproof paper piping bag.

Pour the remaining glacé icing onto the top of the cake and spread almost to the edge with a palette knife. Gently bang the cake on the table 2 or 3 times to help the icing flow to the edge.

Snip the tip off the piping bag and pipe a continuous circular line, starting in the centre of the cake and working towards the outside edge.

Quickly draw a pointed knife from the centre to the edge, marking the cake into quarters. Then draw from edge to centre between the lines to complete the pattern.

Makes one 20 cm (8 inch) cake

Lemon Cake

4-egg lemon-
   flavoured Whisked
   sponge cake
   mixture*
6 tablespoons lemon
   curd
300 g (10 oz)
   yellow Glacé icing
   (see page 9)
yellow and orange
   food colouring
TO DECORATE:
25 g (1 oz) yellow
   desiccated coconut
   (see page 14)
sugar flowers

Line and grease a 23 cm (9 inch)
round cake tin. Turn the mixture
into the tin and bake in a preheated
moderately hot oven, 190°C (375°F),
Gas Mark 5, for 30 to 35 minutes.
Turn onto a wire rack to cool.

Cut the cake in half and sandwich
together with 4 tablespoons of the
lemon curd. Spread the remaining
lemon curd around the side of the
cake, then roll in the coloured
coconut. Place on a cake board.

Pour three-quarters of the glacé
icing onto the top of the cake and
spread almost to the edge with a
palette knife. Gently bang the cake
2 or 3 times on the table to help the
icing flow to the edge. Leave to dry.

Colour the remaining icing with a
few more drops of yellow and a drop
of orange colouring. With a No. 2
writing nozzle pipe lines across the
top of the cake. Pipe across the first
lines to form diamonds. Leave to set
then place a flower in each one.
Makes one 23 cm (9 inch) cake

Mocha Gâteau

3-egg coffee-
   flavoured Whisked
   sponge mixture*
250 g (8 oz)
   chocolate Butter
   icing (see page 11)
75 g (3 oz) plain
   chocolate, grated
chocolate buttons to
   decorate

Line and grease a 20 × 30 cm
(8 × 12 inch) Swiss roll tin. Turn the
mixture into the tin and bake in a
preheated moderately hot oven,
190°C (375°F), Gas Mark 5, for 20 to
25 minutes. Cool on a wire rack.

Cut the cake into 3 equal pieces and
sandwich together with one third of
the butter icing. Spread more icing
over the sides, then coat with grated
chocolate. Place on a cake board.

Spread more icing over the top and
mark with a palette knife. Using the
remaining icing and a fluted nozzle,
pipe a border along the edges of the
cake. Top with chocolate buttons.
Makes one 20 cm (8 inch) gâteau

ELABORATE CAKE DECORATING

Having mastered the simple icings, you will probably want to try your hand at something slightly more complicated. It is only practice that will give good results, but once learned, icing is a skill that will always be useful.

The icings given in this chapter are used for covering large and small sponge cakes; they could also be used to cover a rich fruit cake if it is coated with almond paste. The finished icing on sponge cakes will be improved if the cake is first brushed with apricot glaze (see page 14).

Satin and moulding icings are also used to make moulded decorations, which add a really professional touch to the finished cake.

Fondant Icing

150 ml (¼ pint)
    water
500 g (1 lb)
    granulated or cube
    sugar
1 tablespoon liquid
    glucose
flavouring (see
    below) or few
    drops of food
    colouring
    (optional)

Heat the water and sugar in a heavy-based pan gently until dissolved. Bring to the boil slowly then add the glucose. Boil until the syrup registers 115°C (240°F) on a sugar thermometer.

When the bubbles subside, pour one third into a bowl and the remainder into a separate bowl. Cool until a skin forms.

Working the smaller quantity first, beat with a wooden spoon until thick and white. It will change from a liquid to a paste and finally to a solid white mass. Knead with the fingers, until smooth.

Shape into pieces, the size of a golf ball. Repeat with the larger quantity of fondant. If stored in an airtight jar, this icing will keep for up to 2 months.

To use, place 3 or 4 pieces in a basin over a pan of hot water. Warm gently, stirring, until the fondant is smooth and the consistency of thick cream. Add flavouring or colouring if using. If the icing is too thick, add a little water.

This quantity is sufficient to cover a 20 cm (8 inch) round cake.

Makes a 500 g (1 lb) mixture

FLAVOURINGS

Coffee: Add 2 teaspoons coffee essence.

Chocolate: Blend 1 tablespoon cocoa with 1 tablespoon boiling water. Cool before adding.

Satin Icing

50 g (2 oz) butter or
   margarine
4 tablespoons lemon
   juice
675 g (1½ lb) icing
   sugar, sifted
   (approximately)
few drops of food
   colouring
   (optional)

Warm the fat and lemon juice in a pan
until melted. Add 250 g (8 oz) of the
icing sugar and heat gently, stirring,
until dissolved. When the mixture
begins to simmer at the sides of the
pan, increase the heat slightly and
cook for 2 minutes until it boils
gently; do not overboil at this stage or
the icing will be too hard.

Remove from the heat and add
250 g (8 oz) of the icing sugar. Beat
thoroughly with a wooden spoon,
then turn into a mixing bowl.

Gradually mix in enough of the
remaining icing sugar to give a soft
dough. Turn onto a surface dusted
with icing sugar and knead until
smooth, adding colouring if using.

Wrap in cling film. This icing will
keep in the refrigerator for up to
6 weeks.

Use to mould decorations or to
cover the top and sides of a cake. This
quantity is sufficient to cover a 23 cm
(9 inch) round cake.

Makes a 675 g (1½ lb) mixture

Moulding Icing

1 egg white
1 rounded tablespoon
    liquid glucose
500 g (1 lb) icing
    sugar, sifted
    (approximately)
few drops of food
    colouring
    (optional)

Mix the egg white and glucose together in a basin. Gradually add enough icing sugar to form a stiff paste. Turn onto a surface sprinkled with cornflour and knead until smooth.

Wrap in cling film and keep in a plastic bag to prevent it from drying. The icing will keep in the refrigerator for up to 6 weeks. If the icing does become dry, dip it in hot water, wrap and return to the bag for 1 hour then knead again, adding colouring if using.

Use to mould decorations or to cover the top and sides of a cake. This quantity is sufficient to cover a 20 cm (8 inch) round cake.

Makes a 500 g (1 lb) mixture

27

MOULDED DECORATIONS

Moulding icing is an extremely pliable icing suitable for making flowers and other cake decorations. It holds its shape even when paper thin, and as it is white it is easy to achieve natural colours. Food colourings can be kneaded into the icing or painted on the finished decoration. Keep the icing to be moulded wrapped in a polythene bag as it dries quickly if exposed to air. Leave the decoration for 24 hours to dry and harden.

Rose

Make a cone with a small piece of icing and press out the base to form a stand. Take a piece of icing the size of a pea, dip in cornflour and roll into a ball in the palm of your hand. Using a hard-boiled egg, flatten the icing in your hand with quick gentle strokes, using more cornflour if it is too sticky. The edges of the petal should be paper thin.

Carefully wrap the petal around the cone, turning the edges outwards. Repeat, overlapping each petal, until the desired shape is achieved, using a cocktail stick if necessary to help mould the petals. Leave to dry overnight then cut off the base. When using several roses together in a decoration, colour some a shade darker for a more elaborate effect.

Daisy

Make a small ball of icing and pinch the bottom to form a base. Flatten the ball (as for the rose) to make a thin round. Using small scissors, cut the edges of the round to form petals, then turn them upwards. Using a cocktail stick, make holes in the centre then paint with yellow food colouring. Using pink food colouring and a fine paintbrush, paint the tips of the petals. Leave to dry.

Leaves

Colour the icing green and roll out the icing thinly on a surface dusted with corn-flour. Cut into leaf shapes with a small knife. Lift into the palm of your hand, flatten the edges (as for the rose) and pinch each end into a point. Leave to dry overnight.

Mark veins on each leaf, using a fine paintbrush or the point of a knife dipped into colouring.

Rabbit

Mould a piece of icing into an egg shape. Mould a smaller piece into an oval and place on top of the narrow end of the egg shape to form the head. Shape 2 large ears and attach to the head. Shape a small ball of icing for the tail and attach. Paint the inside of the ears with a little pink colouring. Using pink royal icing* and a No. 1 writing nozzle, pipe on the eyes.

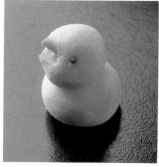

Chick

Shape two balls of yellow icing, one half the size of the other. Stick the small ball on top of the large one for the head. Using small scissors, snip the small ball to form a beak shape and paint the mouth with yellow colouring. Position coloured sugar balls for the eyes.

Mouse

Mould a piece of icing into a cone shape for the body. Shape 2 pieces of icing into ears and stick onto the pointed end, which will be the head. Roll a small piece of icing into a thin tail and stick onto the rounded end of the body. Using royal icing* and a No. 1 nozzle, pipe on eyes.

ALMOND PASTE DECORATIONS

Almond paste used for modelling must be supple enough to bend without cracking, but firm enough to hold its shape. Bought ready-made marzipan is ideal to use for making decorations as you can simply break off the amount you need. If using homemade almond paste, make a large quantity and keep it in a polythene bag, breaking off small amounts as you need them; it will keep for several weeks. Care must be taken not to over-knead, as this will make the paste oily and difficult to handle.

To colour the paste, add a little food colouring at a time, kneading in until it is evenly coloured. Keep the paste not being worked in a polythene bag, as it dries out quickly if exposed to air. Leave the decorations for 2 to 3 days to dry before positioning on the cake. Alternatively make up to 4 weeks in advance and store in an airtight tin.

Oranges and Lemons

Colour some paste orange or lemon. Roll into a ball for an orange and a plump oval for a lemon. Roll over the fine surface of a grater to get the texture of the skin. Press in a clove at one end for the calyx.

Bananas

Colour some paste yellow and form into a banana shape. Paint with brown colouring to represent the skin.

Apples

Colour some paste green and roll into a ball, making a slight indent at the top and base. Cut a clove in half and use the top for the calyx and the rest for the stalk. Paint pink colouring on one side, gradually blending it into the green.

Valentine Cake

4-egg plain or pink
  Victoria sandwich
  cake mixture*
125 g (4 oz)
  strawberry jam
125 g (4 oz) Apricot
  glaze (see page
  14)
500 g (1 lb) pink
  Satin icing (see
  page 26)
125 g (4 oz) Royal
  icing*
pink moulded roses
  (see page 28) to
  decorate

Line and grease a 20 cm (8 inch) heart-shaped cake tin. Turn the mixture into the tin and bake in a preheated moderate oven, 180°C (350°F), Gas Mark 4, for 1½ to 1¾ hours. Turn onto a wire rack to cool.

Cut the cake in half and sandwich together with the jam. Place on a cake board and brush the top and sides with the apricot glaze.

Turn the satin icing onto a surface dusted with icing sugar. Roll out thinly then lift onto the rolling pin and place over the top of the cake. Dip your hands in icing sugar and press the icing onto the cake by rubbing the surface with a circular movement. Work the surplus icing to the base of the cake and cut off.

Put the royal icing into a grease-proof paper piping bag fitted with a No. 2 writing nozzle and pipe a line 1 cm (½ inch) in from the edge of the cake. Pipe dots on each side of the line. Decorate the top with roses.

Makes one valentine cake

Equipment

As well as the basic equipment already described (see page 6), there are some additional pieces of equipment which you will find helpful when using royal icing. Most of these can be obtained from kitchenware shops, but a wider range is available from cake decorating schools.

An *icing turntable*, though not essential, does give a better result for the sides of the cake.

An *icing ruler* is essential for a smooth finish on the top of a cake. Both plastic and stainless steel ones are available.

An *icing scraper* or *comb* makes smoothing the sides of the cake much easier.

A *greaseproof paper* piping bag is the simplest to use for royal icing. If you are using different nozzles or icing a large cake it's a good idea to make several (see page 7). If you use a nylon piping bag, you will need a collar and connector; insert the connector into the bag and screw the nozzle onto the connector.

A good selection of *piping nozzles* makes icing more fun and provides more scope for design.

A *piping nail* is essential when making piped flowers.

Waxed paper is the best to use for run-outs or piping flowers, though silicone paper can also be used.

A *compass* is useful when making circular designs.

Thick *cake boards* are used for royal iced cakes. The cake should be placed on a board 5 cm (2 inches) larger than the cake; for the bottom tier of a wedding cake the board can be up to 10 cm (4 inches) larger.

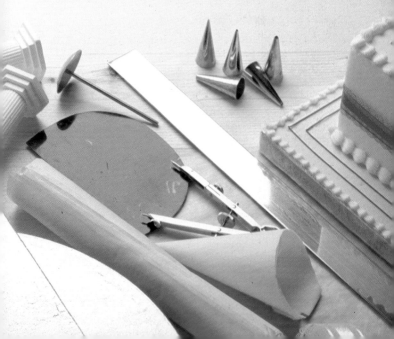

COVERING WITH ALMOND PASTE

Almond paste is used to cover rich fruit cakes before covering with royal, moulding or satin icing. It gives a smooth finish on which to work and prevents the icing being discoloured by the moisture from the cake.

After covering the cake with almond paste, leave to dry at room temperature for 2 to 3 days. If a finished cake is going to be stored for a long time, leave the paste to dry for 5 to 7 days before icing is applied.

For quantities and instructions for making almond paste, see pages 89 to 91.

To cover the top of the cake: Sift a little icing sugar onto a work surface. Roll out half the almond paste to a 1 cm (½ inch) thickness and a square or circle 1 cm (½ inch) larger than the top of the cake.

Brush the top of the cake with apricot glaze (see page 14) and place the cake upside down on the paste. Using a small palette knife, draw up the edge of the paste level to the side of the cake. Smooth evenly all round, trimming away any surplus paste.

To cover the sides of a square cake: Roll out the remaining paste and cut 4 rectangles to fit each side of the cake. Press them gently onto the cake and smooth the joins together with a small palette knife. Place on a cake board.

To cover the side of a round cake: Brush with apricot glaze. Cut a piece of string the circumference of the cake and another piece of string the exact depth of the cake.

Roll out the remaining paste to a strip to fit exactly round the cake, using the pieces of string as your guide. Trim and roll up like a Swiss roll.

Unroll the strip carefully around the cake. Press ends together with a small palette knife. Place on a cake board.

PIPED DECORATIONS

Miniature bell

Using a No. 4 writing nozzle, pipe a large dot onto waxed paper, a smaller dot on top, then a third even smaller one in one movement. Leave to dry for several hours until the outside is firm and the inside still soft.

waxed paper, pressing the icing out into a bulb shape. Raise the bag a little to form the neck and press again to form the head. Pull off quickly to make the beak.

Using a No. 1 nozzle, pipe the wings and tail onto waxed paper. Allow to dry.

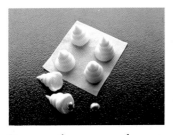

Remove the paper and scoop out the soft icing in the centre to make a thin shell. Secure a silver ball in each bell with a little icing.

Dove

Using a No. 4 writing nozzle, pipe the body onto

When the icing is firm carefully remove the paper. Assemble the sections, securing them with a little icing. Paint in 2 eyes with black food colouring and paint the beak with yellow colouring.

PIPED FLOWERS

To pipe flowers you need a large, medium or fine petal nozzle, depending on the size of flower required; an icing nail; and small squares of waxed paper. Place a little icing on top of the nail and stick a square of waxed paper on top. Leave flowers to dry for 24 hours before removing paper.

Rose

Hold the piping bag with the thin part of the nozzle up. Pipe a cone of icing, twisting the nail quickly between finger and thumb.

Pipe 3 to 5 overlapping petals around the centre of the rose, allowing the outer petals to curve outwards.

Apple Blossom

Working with the thick edge of the nozzle to the centre and keeping it flat, pipe 5 small rounded white petals.

Pipe a yellow dot in the centre. Paint the edges with pink food colouring.

Primrose

Use yellow icing and work with the thick edge of the nozzle to the centre, keeping it flat. Pipe from the centre outwards. Go halfway back in, then out again, then back to the centre to give a heart-shaped petal.

Pipe 5 petals in all. Using a No. 1 writing nozzle, pipe a dot in the middle.

Narcissus

Use yellow icing and work with the thick edge of the nozzle to the centre, keeping it flat. Pipe a petal, then make 5 more petals, starting just under the previous one each time. Leave to dry.

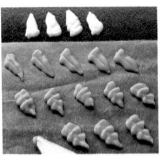

Using a small petal nozzle pipe the centre, twisting the nail quickly to make a complete circle. Paint the edges of the trumpet and petals with yellow food colouring.

Forget-me-nots

These are best piped straight onto the cake. Using a No. 2 writing nozzle and blue icing, pipe 5 or 6 dots touching each other in a circle. Pipe a yellow dot in the centre of each. Pipe curved green lines as stalks.

Leaves

Large leaves may be piped with a leaf nozzle.

A piping bag without a nozzle gives a better effect for smaller leaves. Fill the greaseproof paper bag but don't cut off the tip. Press the tip of the bag flat, then snip off the point in the shape of an arrow. Place the tip of the bag on the paper, holding it at a slight angle. Press out the icing and pull away quickly to make a tapering point. Mark on a vein with a cocktail stick.

Serrated fern-like leaves can be made by moving the tube back and forwards.

When practised, leaves may be piped straight onto the cake.

RUN-OUTS

A run-out is a shaped piece of icing, such as an initial, number, flower, leaf, animal or figure. They can be used for Christmas cake decorations too: Father Christmas, snowmen, robins, Christmas trees, stars, etc.

For a simple run-out shape, pipe the outline straight onto the cake and then flood with icing (see below).

For more difficult shapes, it is easier to pipe the outline onto a piece of waxed paper and then flood with icing. Outlines for Father Christmas, robins and other motifs can be traced from the stencils on pages 92-93. Alternatively, outlines can be traced from designs on Christmas cards.

Run-outs can be stored in an airtight container for a few months without discolouring.

Preparing the shape

Draw or trace the outline onto a piece of card. Secure a piece of waxed paper over the card. Using a No. 2 writing nozzle and icing the same colour as that to be used for flooding, trace the outline of the drawing. Move the waxed paper along over the card to make the required number of shapes; always make more than you need to allow for breakages when removing paper.

Flooding the shape

Thin down a little royal icing with egg white until it is a flowing consistency. Spoon it into the centre of the outline, making a slight dome; if it is a very small area pipe in the icing using a No. 3 writing nozzle. Use a cocktail stick to ease the icing into corners, and to prick any air bubbles. Leave to dry, then pipe in lines or dots to complete the detail of the run-out or paint with food colouring.

Removing the paper

Leave for 2 to 3 days to dry completely then remove the paper: place the run-out on a thick book, slightly overlapping the edge. Pull the paper gently downwards, then turn the run-out round, pulling the paper away until all the edges are loose. Gently pull off the paper. Secure the run-out in position on the cake with a little royal icing.

Butterfly

Outline the wings and body separately. Carefully flood each section with icing and leave to dry.

Pipe 2 antennae with a No. 1 writing nozzle. Decorate the wings with piped lines and dots, using a No. 1 writing nozzle, or paint on with food colouring. Use a little icing to attach the wings and antennae to the body at a slight angle. Hold the wings in position with small pieces of plasticine until dry.

Flowers

Outline the flower. Flood each petal using a No. 3 writing nozzle and leave to dry.

Pipe an outline around each petal and several dots in the centre with a No. 1 writing nozzle. Diluted food colouring may be used to paint the petals, using dark shades in the centre and pale towards the outer edges.

Run-out pansies are extremely pretty, especially when two shades are used in the same flower. Outline the large lower petal in each flower, flood with icing and leave to dry. When set, outline the remaining petals and fill with a lighter shade. To finish, paint streaks from the centre of the petals with food colouring.

Ivy leaves

Outline the leaf, then flood. When dry, use a No. 1 writing nozzle and pipe a thin line of icing down the centre to make a vein and stalk.

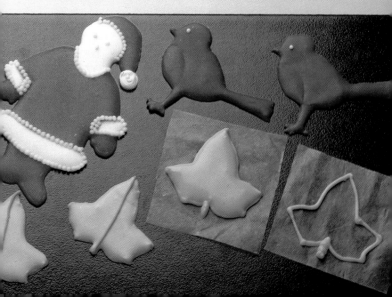

DESIGNING THE CAKE

Most designs on cakes are regular geometric shapes because they ensure the cake will look good from every angle. Once you have mastered the basic techniques, you can create your own designs, getting ideas from cakes in confectioners' windows, wallpapers, pieces of lace, and other sources.

Loops make a very attractive decoration around the sides of a cake. They can be piped simply or elaborated with dots, made with fine, medium and thick writing nozzles, and flowers used singly or in clusters of 3.

Most designs need to be carefully drawn to scale and a template made for accurate marking on the cake.

Making a simple template
For the top: Cut a piece of greaseproof paper the size of the top of the cake. Fold in half 3 times to make a cone shape; crease the edges well. Draw the scallop or desired shape on the paper, using a compass, base of a glass or other suitable object. Prick along the line with a pin right through paper. Open out and secure on top of the cake with pins. Use a pin to

prick along the outline of the design. Remove paper and the design will be marked on the cake.
For the sides: Measure the depth of the cake and cut a band of greaseproof paper to size. Fold it to give the required size and number of scallops, etc. Draw the design on the paper and open out. Secure on top of the cake and mark design with pins as above.

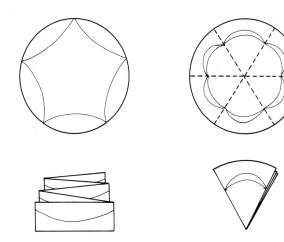

Silver Wedding Cake Templates (recipe, page 61)
For the top: Cut out a 25 cm (10 inch) circle of grease-proof paper and mark 5 equally spaced points on the circumference.

Using a compass or the base of a suitable-sized glass, draw 5 scallops, joining the marks on the paper and making them about 5 cm (2 inches) deep on the curve. Position the template and mark the design as described.

For the side: Measure and cut a band of greaseproof paper as described. Place it around the cake and secure with pins. Mark the points of the scallops already marked on the top of the cake. Remove the paper and draw in the scallops as for the top, but not quite so deep. Secure the band to the cake with pins, placing it a little above centre so that the points of top and side curves almost meet. Mark the design as described.

Rose Wedding Cake Templates (recipe, page 64)
For the top: Cut out and fold 3 greaseproof paper circles as described. Open out and place on the cakes. Using a compass or the base of a suitable sized glass, mark an outward facing scallop between each crease; make the curve about 5 cm (2 inches) in from the side of the larger cake, 2.5 cm (1 inch) in for the middle tier and 1 cm (½ inch) in for the top tier. Remove the paper from the cakes and draw in the design firmly. Position the template and mark the design as described.

For the side: Measure and cut 3 bands of greaseproof paper as described. Fold each into 6 sections. Draw a scallop as described for the top, to correspond with the one on the top of each cake but not quite so deep. Place around the cake, matching the curves on the top. Position the template and mark the design as described.

Christmas Bell Cake

23 cm (9 inch)
  square Rich fruit
  cake, covered with
  almond paste*
900 g (2 lb) white
  Royal icing*
red food colouring
18-20 sugar bells
  (see below)

Cover the cake with 3 layers of royal icing, allowing it to dry between each coat, then ice the board.

Fit a greaseproof paper piping bag with a No. 43 star nozzle and half fill with royal icing. Pipe a row of shells around the top and bottom edges of the cake. Using a No. 44 star nozzle pipe another row of shells around the edge of the board. Colour a little icing red. Fit a greaseproof paper piping bag with a No. 2 writing nozzle and half fill with the red icing. Pipe a line of icing all round the top of the cake inside the shell border. Pipe 2 lines of red icing on the board around the cake.

Arrange a cluster of 3 bells at each corner of the cake on the board. Arrange the remaining bells in a cluster in one top corner of the cake. Write 'Nöel' in the opposite corner. Outline the inner edge of the other corners with 2 right-angled red lines to complete the design. Tie a red ribbon around the cake.

Makes one 23 cm (9 inch) cake

Sugar Bells: Place 2 tablespoons granulated sugar in a basin and gradually mix in a few drops of egg white until the mixture is crumbly. Press into a bell mould, then tip out. Repeat to make 20 bells. Leave to dry.

When the bells are firm to the touch on the outside, but still soft in the centre, scoop out the centres to make the bells as fine as possible.

Pipe a little white royal icing into each bell, using a greaseproof paper piping bag fitted with a No. 1 writing nozzle and press in silver balls.

Sugar bells are fragile and must be handled carefully. Make more than the number required to allow for breakage.

Silver Wedding Anniversary Cake

25 cm (10 inch)
   round Rich fruit
   cake, covered with
   almond paste*
1.25 kg (2½ lb)
   white Royal
   icing*
30 white piped roses
   (see page 50)

Cover the cake with 3 layers of royal icing, allowing it to dry between each coat, then ice the board.

Make a template (see page 55) and mark the design on the cake.

Fit a greaseproof paper piping bag with a No. 2 writing nozzle, half fill with icing and outline the design, covering the pin pricks completely. Using a No. 1 writing nozzle, fill in the scallops with lacework and pipe lacework·on the board.

Pipe '25' in the centre of the cake using a No. 2 writing nozzle. Using a No. 3 writing nozzle, pipe dots around the base of the cake.

Fix the flowers in clusters of 3 between the scallops on the top and side of the cake, with a little icing.

Using a No. 1 writing nozzle, overpipe the 25 on top of the cake. Pipe a loop under each scallop on the side of the cake.

Makes one 25 cm (10 inch) cake

Christening Cake

25 cm (10 inch)
    square Rich fruit
    cake, covered with
    almond paste*
900 g (2 lb) pale
    pink or blue Royal
    icing*
500 g (1 lb) white
    Royal icing*
4 piped doves and 36
    bells (see page
    49)

Cover the cake with 3 layers of pink or blue icing, allowing to dry between each coat, then ice the board.

Using a No. 2 writing nozzle and white icing, pipe a trellis all round the top of the cake, starting 2.5 cm (1 inch) in from the top edge and finishing 1 cm (½ inch) down the side of the cake. Repeat round the bottom and down each corner.

When dry, pipe another trellis on top, using a No. 1 writing nozzle. Allow to dry. Using a No. 1 writing nozzle, join the edges of the trellis on the sides and board with loops.

Using a No. 2 writing nozzle and white icing, pipe 2 curved lines on top of the cake, joining the corners. Finish with a line of dots. Pipe a similar curved design on the sides.

Arrange a dove in each corner and the bells in clusters of 3 around the sides, fixing them with a little icing. Pipe a line of dots below each cluster.

Write the baby's name on the cake in white, using a No. 2 nozzle. Leave to dry, then overpipe with pink or blue icing, using a No. 1 nozzle.

Makes one 25 cm (10 inch) cake

21st Birthday Cake

23 cm (9 inch) round
  Rich fruit cake,
  covered with
  almond paste*
900 g (2 lb) white
  Royal icing*
blue or pink food
  colourings

Cover the cake with 3 layers of royal icing, allowing to dry between each coat, then ice the board. Make a simple top scallop template (see page 54); mark the design on the cake.

Using a No. 2 writing nozzle, outline the design, covering the pin marks completely. Pipe a trellis in each scallop and leave to dry. Colour a little icing blue or pink and pipe over the trellis, using a No. 1 nozzle.

Using a No. 44 star nozzle, pipe a star border around the bottom edge of the cake. Using a No. 42 star nozzle, pipe similar borders around the top of the cake and along the edge of the board.

Pipe evenly spaced white forget-me-nots (see page 51) around the side of the cake and board. Join the flowers with stalks, making a curved design. Pipe a few leaves on the stalks. When dry, overpipe the flowers with blue or pink icing.

Pipe '21' on the cake using white icing and a No. 2 writing nozzle. When dry, overpipe with blue or pink icing, using a No. 1 nozzle.

Makes one 23 cm (9 inch) cake

WEDDING CAKES

When making a wedding cake, it is most important to choose the sizes of the tiers carefully. For a 3-tier cake a good proportion would be 15, 23 and 30 cm (6, 9 and 12 inches). For a 2-tier cake 20 and 30 cm (8 and 12 inches), or 18 and 25 cm (7 and 10 inches), or 15 and 23 cm (6 and 9 inches) would all be suitable.

Ideally, the tiers should vary in depth: the bottom one should be slightly deeper than the middle one, and the middle one slightly deeper than the top one.

When royal icing a tiered wedding cake, omit the glycerine in the royal icing for all tiers except the top one, otherwise the icing will not be firm enough to support the weight of the cakes.

Cake boards should be 5 cm (2 inches) larger than the cakes so they project 2.5 cm (1 inch) all round when the cake is covered with marzipan and icing. The bottom tier looks better on a board 7.5 to 10 cm (3 to 4 inches) larger than the cake.

3-Tier Rose Wedding Cake

1 each 15, 20 and 25 cm (6, 8 and 10 inch) round Rich fruit cakes, covered with almond paste*
2.25 kg (5 lb) white Royal icing*
36 piped white roses and 72 leaves (see page 50)

Cover the cakes with 3 layers of royal icing, allowing it to dry between each coat, then ice the boards.

Make the templates (see page 55) and mark the design on the cakes.

Fit a greaseproof paper piping bag with a No. 2 writing nozzle, half fill with icing and outline the designs, covering the pin pricks completely. Pipe a second line inside the scallop on the top of each cake, and below the scallop on the side. Place a rose and 2 leaves at the point of each scallop, securing with a little icing. Using the same nozzle, pipe dots below each rose on the side.

Fit a greaseproof paper piping bag with a No. 44 star nozzle. Pipe a shell border around the top and bottom edges of each cake.

Assemble the cakes, using 8 white pillars, and place a fresh flower arrangement on top of the cake.
Makes one 3-tier round cake

2-Tier Butterfly Wedding Cake

1 each 18 and 25 cm
(7 and 10 inch)
square Rich fruit
cakes, covered
with almond
paste*
2 kg (4 lb) white
Royal icing*
250 g (8 oz) yellow
Royal icing*
12 white butterfly
run-outs
(see page 53)

Cover the cakes with 3 layers of royal icing, allowing it to dry between each coat, then ice the boards.

Mark the centre point of each side on the top of the cakes. Join by marking a line with a pin to make a diamond shape.

Fit a greaseproof paper piping bag with a No. 2 writing nozzle, half fill with white icing and pipe a line to cover the pin marks. Pipe a trellis in the 4 corners of the cakes. Leave to dry, then using a No. 1 nozzle and yellow icing, cover with a second layer of trellis work. Neaten the edges of the trellis with a row of stars using a No. 42 star nozzle.

Using a No. 44 star nozzle, pipe a star border at the bottom edge of the cakes. Using a No. 42 star nozzle, pipe a star border around the edges of the boards.

Using a No. 2 writing nozzle, pipe 3 looped lines on each side of the cakes, making 2 loops on each side. Pipe a series of dots from the points where the loops meet.

Using the same nozzle, pipe 3 parallel lines on the bottom board and 2 lines on the top one. Overpipe these lines and the dots with yellow icing, using a No. 1 nozzle.

Using the yellow icing and a No. 1 writing nozzle, outline the butterflies and pipe dots around the wings. Leave to dry. Place a butterfly at each corner of the boards. Arrange butterflies at the points of the diamonds on the larger cake.

Assemble the cakes using 4 white pillars and place a fresh flower arrangement on the top of the cake.
Makes one 2-tier square cake

NOVELTY CAKES

It is difficult at a children's party to focus attention on the birthday cake when there are so many other goodies on the table. One way of overcoming this is to produce a novelty cake; it can be a simple round sponge, decorated as a clock, drum or maypole, but still effective. Or it can be a more unusual and exciting cake.

If you choose a design that requires cutting to shape, make the cake the day before so that it is not too crumbly; a Victoria sandwich cake is the easiest to cut. To avoid the crumbs getting mixed in with the icing and spoiling the finished effect, brush the cake with apricot glaze first.

The decorations can almost always be sweets but a little simple piping is sometimes needed to give the best result.

Large cake boards are useful as bases for the cakes, though a chopping board covered in foil makes a good substitute. Alternatively novelty cakes may be placed on thin cake cards onto which they fit exactly.

Clock Cake

4-egg Victoria
    sandwich cake
    mixture*
175 g (6 oz)
    chocolate Butter
    icing (see page 11)
2 × 100 g (3½ oz)
    packets milk
    chocolate finger
    biscuits
250 g (8 oz) Glacé
    icing (see page 9)
1 teaspoon cocoa
    powder

Line and grease two 20 cm (8 inch)
sandwich tins. Turn the mixture into
the tins and bake in a preheated
moderate oven, 180°C (350°F), Gas
Mark 4, for 30 to 35 minutes. Turn
onto a wire rack to cool.

Sandwich the cakes together with
three quarters of the butter icing.
Cover the sides with the remaining
butter icing and place on a board.
Trim the chocolate fingers to the
height of the cake and arrange
around the edge.

Spread three quarters of the glacé
icing over the top of the cake and
leave to set. Add the cocoa to the
remaining glacé icing and put into a
greaseproof paper piping bag fitted
with a No. 2 writing nozzle.

Pipe a circle of dots around the top
of the cake. Pipe on the clock
numbers and the hands, pointing to
the o'clock corresponding with the
child's age.

Makes one 'clock'

Fairy Castle

6-egg Victoria
    sandwich cake
    mixture*
1 packet lemon jelly
blue food colouring
350 g (12 oz) Butter
    icing (see page 11)
3 tablespoons Apricot
    glaze (see page 14)
4 round ice cream
    cones
2 miniature Swiss
    rolls
2 large Swiss rolls
½ wagon wheel
sugar strands
175 g (6 oz) white
    Glacé icing (see
    page 9)
2 ice cream wafers
125 g (4 oz) bar
    nougat, cut into
    small rectangles
sugar flowers
50 g (2 oz) green
    Glacé icing (see
    page 9)

diagram 1

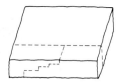

diagram 2

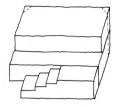

Line and grease two deep 20 cm
(8 inch) square cake tins. Divide the
mixture between them. Bake in a
preheated moderate oven, 180°C
(350°F), Gas Mark 4, for 1 to 1¼
hours. Cool on a wire rack.

Make up the jelly, adding blue
colouring while it is still liquid.

Cut a 5 cm (2 inch) slice from one
cake and cut steps (see diagram 1).
Stick onto one side of the larger cake
with butter icing. Sandwich the cakes
together with butter icing as shown
in diagram 2. Trim a 2.5 cm (1 inch)
triangular section from each rear
corner. Brush cake with apricot glaze.

Trim 2.5 cm (1 inch) from the top
of 2 ice cream cones; discard. Cover
the miniature Swiss rolls, the 4 cones
and sides of the cake with butter icing.

Colour three quarters of the
remaining butter icing blue. Use to
cover the large Swiss rolls and
wagon wheel. Place the rolls at the
rear corners of the cake and the
wagon wheel at the front.

Place the small rolls at the front
corners and top with the small cones.
Place the larger cones on the rear
Swiss rolls. Cover the front, back,
platform and steps with blue icing.
Sprinkle sugar strands over the steps.

Pour the white glacé icing on top
of the cake and spread to the edges.
Shape the wafers to make doors and
windows; press into position.
Arrange the nougat pieces to
represent battlements. Decorate the
walls with sugar flowers. Pipe on
stalks, using the green glacé icing.

Pipe borders around the spires and
door with the remaining white
butter icing. Chop the jelly and
arrange around the castle as a moat.
Makes one 'fairy castle'

Kitten

4-egg chocolate
    Victoria sandwich
    cake mixture*
350 g (12 oz)
    chocolate Butter
    icing (see page 11)
3 sponge fingers
2 ice cream cones
few liquorice sweets
1 piece red liquorice
    ribbon
few short pieces
    spaghetti

Grease and line a 600 ml (1 pint) and
a 1.2 litre (2 pint) ovenproof pudding
basin and two-thirds fill each basin
with the mixture. Bake in a preheated
moderate oven, 180°C (350°F), Gas
Mark 4, for 1 hour for the small cake
and 1¼ to 1½ hours for the large
one. Turn onto a wire rack to cool.

Trim the small cake into a ball for
the head. Trim a slice from one side
of the large cake to flatten the chest.
Place the large cake on a cake board
and fix the small one on top with a
little butter icing. Position a sponge
finger at the side for a tail.

Cut a 1 cm (½ inch) slice off the
other sponge fingers. Place them
either side of the chest, as legs;
position the slices as paws. Cut the
tips off the ice cream cones and place
on either side of the head for ears.

Cover the kitten with the icing.
Shape the sweets for the eyes and
nose; press into position. Tie the
liquorice round the neck in a bow
and position the spaghetti as whiskers.
Makes one 'kitten'

REFERENCE SECTION

These three recipes have been used for all the cakes in the book. To some extent they are inter-changeable, but for novelty cakes, where shaping is involved, a Victoria sandwich cake is the most suitable.

Victoria Sandwich Cake

This is referred to as a 2-egg mixture. For larger quantities, simply increase the ingredients in proportion.

125 g (4 oz) butter or margarine
125 g (4 oz) caster sugar
2 eggs
125 g (4 oz) self-raising flour, sifted
1 tablespoon hot water

Line and grease the baking tin(s).

Cream the fat and sugar together until light and fluffy. Beat in the eggs one at a time, adding a tablespoon of the flour with the second egg. Fold in the remaining flour with a metal spoon, then the hot water.

Turn the mixture into the prepared tin(s) and bake in a preheated moderate oven, 180°C (350°F), Gas Mark 4, for the required time, until the cake springs back when lightly pressed. Turn onto a wire rack to cool.

VARIATIONS

Chocolate: Blend 1 tablespoon cocoa powder with 1 tablespoon hot water. Cool slightly then beat in with the fat and sugar.

Coffee: Add 1 tablespoon instant coffee powder with the flour.

Orange or Lemon: Add the grated rind of 1 orange or lemon with the fat and sugar. Replace the water with orange or lemon juice.

Pink: Add a few drops of food colouring to the hot water before folding into the mixture.

Whisked Sponge Cake

This is referred to as a 3-egg mixture. For larger quantities, increase the ingredients in proportion.

3 eggs
140 g (4½ oz) caster sugar
75 g (3 oz) plain flour, sifted

Line, grease and flour the baking tin(s).

Place the eggs and sugar in a heatproof bowl over a pan of boiling water and whisk until the mixture is thick and pale and leaves a trail when the whisk is lifted. (The hot water is unnecessary if using an electric beater.)

Fold in the flour with a metal spoon, then turn into the prepared tin(s). Bake in a preheated moderately hot oven, 190°C (375°F), Gas Mark 5, for the required time, until the cake springs back when lightly pressed. Turn onto a wire rack to cool.

VARIATIONS

Chocolate: Replace 25 g (1 oz) flour with cocoa powder; sift with the flour.

Lemon or Orange: Whisk in the grated rind of 1 lemon or orange with the eggs and sugar.

Coffee: Add 1 tablespoon instant coffee powder with the flour.

RICH FRUIT CAKE

For the ingredients, see quantity chart on pages 90-91.

Grease the inside of the tin. Line the base and sides with a double layer of greaseproof paper, allowing it to extend 5 cm (2 inches) above the rim. Grease well. Tie a thick band of newspaper around the outside of the tin. Stand on a pad of newspaper on a baking sheet.

Sift the flour and spices together. Cream the fat and sugar and lemon rind together until light and fluffy. Beat in the treacle. Beat in the eggs one at a time, adding a tablespoon of flour with all but the first. Fold in the remaining flour, the ground almonds, fruit and nuts until thoroughly mixed.

Turn the mixture into the prepared tin(s) and smooth the top with the back of a spoon. Bake on the middle shelf of a preheated cool oven, 140°C (275°F), Gas Mark 1.

Test the smallest 3 cake sizes given in the chart after 3 hours, the larger sizes after 3½ to 4 hours. If a skewer inserted into the centre comes out clean, it is cooked. If not, return the cake to the oven and test again at 30 minute intervals.

Leave in the tin(s) for 30 minutes, then turn onto a wire rack to cool.

Prick the cake with a skewer and spoon the brandy over the surface; this helps to increase the storage time and keeps the cake moist.

Wrap the cake in greaseproof paper and then a double thickness of foil. Store in a cool dry place for 2 to 3 months to mature, before covering with almond paste.

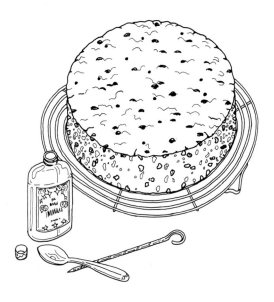

ALMOND PASTE

For the ingredients see the quantity chart on pages 90-91.

Mix the almonds and sugars together in a mixing bowl and make a well in the centre. Add the lemon juice, almond essence and enough egg yolk or beaten egg to mix to a firm paste.

Turn onto a surface sprinkled with icing sugar and knead lightly until smooth; do not over-knead or the paste will become oily and difficult to handle. Keep in a polythene bag until required as almond paste dries out quickly if exposed to air.

Note: When a recipe calls for a given quantity of paste, e.g. Simnel Cake, this is the total weight of the paste. To obtain the weight required use half ground almonds to a quarter each icing and caster sugar.

Ready-made Almond Paste or Marzipan

This can be used instead of home-made almond paste for convenience, although it does not have quite the same flavour. To obtain the amount required for a certain sized cake, simply add the weight of the ground almonds and sugars given in the almond paste chart for that cake size.

ROYAL ICING

For the ingredients, see the quantity chart on pages 90-91.

Beat the egg whites with a fork until frothy. Gradually beat in half the icing sugar, using a wooden spoon. Beat in half the remaining icing sugar with the glycerine, if using, and lemon juice. Beat thoroughly until smooth and white. Beat in enough of the remaining icing sugar to give a consistency that stands in soft peaks. Add colouring if required.

Cover the bowl with a damp cloth and leave to stand for several hours to allow any air bubbles to rise to the surface and burst. Before using stir well with a wooden spoon; do not overbeat.

If using an electric mixer, use on the slowest speed and leave the icing to stand for 24 hours as it will incorporate more air which needs longer to disperse. If air pockets are not dispersed, they will cause breaks in the icing during piping.

Note: If a recipe calls for a given quantity of royal icing, this refers to the amount of icing sugar used. For each 250 g (8 oz) icing sugar, 1 egg white is required.

Using Royal Icing

The required consistency of royal icing depends upon its use. For flat icing or piping rosettes it should be fairly firm. For piping lattice work or writing it should be a little thinner. For run-outs it will need to be thinned with a little lightly beaten egg white to flood the shapes.

Quantity Chart for Rich Fruit Cake

Round	15 cm (6 inch)	18 cm (7 inch)	20 cm (8 inch)
Square	13 cm (5 inch)	15 cm (6 inch)	18 cm (7 inch)
Plain flour	125 g (4 oz)	175 g (6 oz)	200 g (7 oz)
Ground mixed spice	½ teaspoon	1 teaspoon	1 teaspoon
Ground nutmeg	good pinch	½ teaspoon	½ teaspoon
Butter or margarine	100 g (3½ oz)	150 g (5 oz)	175 g (6 oz)
Soft brown sugar	100 g (3½ oz)	150 g (5 oz)	175 g (6 oz)
Grated lemon rind	½ lemon	1 lemon	1 lemon
Black treacle	½ tablespoon	1 tablespoon	1 tablespoon
Eggs	2 large	3 large	4 large
Ground almonds	25 g (1 oz)	40 g (1½ oz)	50 g (2 oz)
Currants	175 g (6 oz)	250 g (8 oz)	300 g (10 oz)
Sultanas	125 g (4 oz)	150 g (5 oz)	200 g (7 oz)
Raisins	50 g (2 oz)	75 g (3 oz)	125 g (4 oz)
Glacé cherries	40 g (1½ oz)	50 g (2 oz)	65 g (2½ oz)
Mixed peel	40 g (1½ oz)	50 g (2 oz)	65 g (2½ oz)
Blanched almonds	40 g (1½ oz)	50 g (2 oz)	65 g (2½ oz)
Brandy	1 tablespoon	1 tablespoon	2 tablespoons

Quantity Chart for Almond Paste

Round	15 cm (6 inch)	18 cm (7 inch)	20 cm (8 inch)
Square	13 cm (5 inch)	15 cm (6 inch)	18 cm (7 inch)
Ground almonds	175 g (6 oz)	250 g (8 oz)	350 g (12 oz)
Caster sugar	75 g (3 oz)	125 g (4 oz)	175 g (6 oz)
Icing sugar	75 g (3 oz)	125 g (4 oz)	175 g (6 oz)
Lemon juice	1 teaspoon	1 teaspoon	2 teaspoons
Almond essence	2 drops	2 drops	3 drops
Eggs	1 yolk	1 standard	1 standard

Quantity Chart for Royal Icing

Round	15 cm (6 inch)	18 cm (7 inch)	20 cm (8 inch)
Square	13 cm (5 inch)	15 cm (6 inch)	18 cm (7 inch)
Egg whites	2	2	3
Icing sugar	500 g (1 lb)	625 g (1¼ lb)	750 g (1½ lb)
Lemon juice	1 teaspoon	1 teaspoon	1 teaspoon
Glycerine (optional)	1 teaspoon	1 teaspoon	1½ teaspoons

These quantities are sufficient for applying two coats of royal icing and simple decoration.

23 cm (9 inch)	25 cm (10 inch)	28 cm (11 inch)	30 cm (12 inch)
20 cm (8 inch)	23 cm (9 inch)	25 cm (10 inch)	28 cm (11 inch)
275 g (9 oz)	325 g (11 oz)	400 g (14 oz)	500 g (1 lb)
1 ½ teaspoons	1 ½ teaspoons	2 teaspoons	2 teaspoons
½ teaspoon	½ teaspoon	½ teaspoon	1 teaspoon
250 g (8 oz)	300 g (10 oz)	350 g (12 oz)	400 g (14 oz)
250 g (8 oz)	300 g (10 oz)	350 g (12 oz)	400 g (14 oz)
1 lemon	1 lemon	2 lemons	2 lemons
1 tablespoon	2 tablespoons	2 tablespoons	2 tablespoons
5 large	6 large	7 large	8 large
65 g (2 ½ oz)	75 g (3 oz)	100 g (3 ½ oz)	125 g (4 oz)
375 g (13 oz)	500 g (1 lb)	625 g (1 ¼ lb)	750 g (1 ½ lb)
275 g (9 oz)	325 g (11 oz)	375 g (13 oz)	500 g (1 lb)
150 g (5 oz)	175 g (6 oz)	200 g (7 oz)	250 g (8 oz)
100 g (3 ½ oz)	125 g (4 oz)	150 g (5 oz)	175 g (6 oz)
100 g (3 ½ oz)	125 g (4 oz)	150 g (5 oz)	175 g (6 oz)
100 g (3 ½ oz)	125 g (4 oz)	150 g (5 oz)	175 g (6 oz)
2 tablespoons	3 tablespoons	3 tablespoons	4 tablespoons

23 cm (9 inch)	25 cm (10 inch)	28 cm (11 inch)	30 cm (12 inch)
20 cm (8 inch)	23 cm (9 inch)	25 cm (10 inch)	28 cm (11 inch)
500 g (1 lb)	625 g (1 ¼ lb)	750 g (1 ½ lb)	850 g (1 ¾ lb)
250 g (8 oz)	300 g (10 oz)	350 g (12 oz)	400 g (14 oz)
250 g (8 oz)	300 g (10 oz)	350 g (12 oz)	400 g (14 oz)
2 teaspoons	3 teaspoons	3 teaspoons	4 teaspoons
3 drops	½ teaspoon	½ teaspoon	1 teaspoon
1 large	2 large	2 large + 1 yolk	3 large

23 cm (9 inch)	25 cm (10 inch)	28 cm (11 inch)	30 cm (12 inch)
20 cm (8 inch)	23 cm (9 inch)	25 cm (10 inch)	28 cm (11 inch)
3	4	4	5
850 g (1 ¾ lb)	1 kg (2 lb)	1 kg (2 lb)	1.5 kg (3 lb)
2 teaspoons	2 teaspoons	2 teaspoons	3 teaspoons
1 ½ teaspoons	2 teaspoons	2 teaspoons	3 teaspoons

DECORATION TEMPLATES

INDEX

Acknowledgments

Photography by Paul Williams
Food prepared by Carole Handslip

The publishers would also like to thank
Baker Smith (Cake Decorating Equipment) Limited and
Margaret Patchin for help with photography.

Specialist suppliers:

Baker Smith Ltd
65 The Street
Tongham
Farnham
Surrey

Mary Ford Cake Artistry Centre
28–30 Southbourne Grove
Bournemouth
Dorset